MW01092993

Words in Silence

Liber Silentis

Words in Silence

Order of Aset Ka

LUIS MARQUES

Words in Silence – Liber Silentis

Luis Marques

Words by Luis Marques
Artwork by Tânia Fonseca
Photography by McGunnMedia

Published and edited in Portugal by Aset Ka

Apartado 52230

4202-803 Porto, Portugal

ASETKA

To contact the author, mail can be sent to the publisher's address using the author's name, as recipient, and the contents will be forwarded. The Aset Ka will not guarantee that every letter written to the author will be answered, but all will be forwarded.

First Edition published in 2014.
ISBN 978-989-95694-3-0

Any copy of this work issued by the publisher as a paperback is sold subject to the condition that it shall not by way of trade or otherwise be lent, resold, hired out or otherwise circulated without the publisher's prior consent in any form of binding or cover other than that in which it is published and without a similar condition including these words being imposed on a subsequent purchaser.

Copyright © 2014 Luis Marques.
All rights reserved. No part of this publication may be reproduced or transmitted in any form and by any means without prior permission from the Aset Ka and Luis Marques. Short passages and transcripts can be quoted on reviews or essays, if the source is explicitly cited.

Kemetic Order of Aset Ka
www.asetka.org
public@asetka.org

Contents

Disclaimer

Asetians are by no means harmless beings or the personification of kindness. They do not abide by social standards nor fall under the understanding of the common mind. In the silence and darkness of their inscrutable nature they are known not to be social and often do not nurture an inborn friendliness over society. Their ageless culture is built upon predatory occultism, the dark arts, a powerful layer of spirituality and secrets long forgotten to mankind.

In their dual essence and misunderstood existence, as elemental forces of nature, the Asetians may be gentle, loving and protective, being capable of the most selfless acts of healing and nobility, while also wielding a devastating side that can be fierce, unforgiving and horrifying. However, awareness of this fact does not mean that an Asetian mind is something that you should fearfully run away from. Their legacy echoes a culture that teaches spiritual growth, learning and evolution; that fights stagnation, dishonesty and weakness. They, above all, protect wisdom, shield innocence and enforce loyalty, honor and union. Asetians are the craftsmen of the subtle, the swordsmen of magick and the scholars of arcane wisdom.

But… is it dangerous to study Asetian knowledge?

✝

For the immature and ignorant-minded, the obsessive, compulsive and paranoid; for the weak, the numb and the slow; the ones drowned in a crown of ego or enslaved by a desire of vanity; for those that do not perpetually question the mystical details in life and challenge their own reality; the ones who believe in religion and dogma out of everything that is pushed down their throats; for the disrespectful and arrogant towards everything that they do not know and fear; to all those people... yes, Asetian spirituality is and always will be a very dangerous subject to study and get involved with.

The Order of Aset Ka will not be held responsible for what use is made with the information provided within their work, texts, teachings and practices. The occult science of the Asetians is an expression of the timeless voice of nature that unveils the secret keys to the fabric of immortal consciousness, and as such it is bound to the exercise of responsibility. The potential danger in its misuse is undeniable.

This book was designed for Asetians and the followers of the violet path, but everyone from any walk of life is welcome to read, meditate and question this work. Just keep an open and sharp mind.

Welcome to our world...

Introduction

𝓔m 𝓗otep.

Words are magick. That was the belief of the Ancient
Egyptians; a spiritual and metaphysical paradigm that
stood at the core of ancient wisdom. Such esoteric science
of the elders was a powerful vehicle for the passing of
hidden teachings – the mysteries. Bound to a code of
secrecy that could shield them from those who seek to
destroy, deface and exploit such powers, the magickal
words were encrypted in the language of symbolism,
intuition and energy. It became a subtle lock that could
only be opened through a natural process of initiation into
the Asetian realm.

For the past five years I have crafted a system of
utterances that are limited in length but unlimited in

scope of magickal reach. They elaborate on a series of teachings that are, in my opinion, essential to the evolution of the soul on its road of growth in the physical realm – the incarnated reality – and embody different layers of Asetian understanding, the ancient wisdom of the Aset Ka and elements that define the body of gnosis, ideals and values within this path. The individual sentences are literarily encoded in the depths of symbolism and the demonic mirrors of the unconscious mind, providing a fragment of wisdom that should be carefully studied under awareness towards the multitude of possible interpretations, though not all are intentionally cryptic or spellbinding. Some are surprisingly simple and yet effective in what they intend to convey while few are taken directly from other Asetian texts of my authorship such as the Book of Orion, the Asetian Bible and other private and even unpublished works. Their latent potential and the magnitude of the consequential magickal results achieved by the adept will be intimately bound to the strength of the fabric that makes up the student himself; as with most of my teachings, the profound lessons and their innermost powers can only be found by those who persevere. Do not be fooled by the apparently simplistic structure of this tome as an organized tapestry of spiritual sentences and its multilayered cobweb of occult lessons and magickal utterances. Such content is much more than a mere compilation of ideas or a numbered listing of phrases – it is a manual for the perilous journey within. The wise allowing its guidance and the humble studying its lessons will discover magickal keys that have the ability to open different doors of power, knowledge and understanding, but not all will be able to read between the lines and make enlightened use of its symbolism. Upon this inked map of words, thoughts and energy, some will inevitably fall, never to rise again, while others shall find the strength to proceed, to conquer and to overcome. There will be sadness but there will also be happiness. There will be pain and there will be pleasure. Fear that can only be conquered with a sword. Craft your inner boat and sail the mysterious river of Asetianism with determination, honor and loyalty. When others fall down from their misshapen boats and become prey to the crocodiles lurking in this river, or those lacking the tools of evolution required to craft the first boat and start their journey, or even those too scared, too lazy or too limited to seek the crafting tools themselves, they all shall see this book as nothing more than a simple list of confusing statements and cryptic thoughts. Do not feed the crocodiles and do not stare them in the eye.

It becomes increasingly important to understand that the broad and multilayered field of the occult includes more than the exploration and mastery of magick. Occult knowledge and expertise manifests beyond the perception of hidden forces and the attaining of mystical wisdom. One important aspect of this path is the in-depth study of the mind, in its many manifestations and profound complexities – a process that can reach deeper than the limited scope of modern psychology, providing answers and a high level of understanding often not at the reach of someone imposing barriers on the exploration of something as limitless as the incredible potential of the mind. Such study has been a personal interest of mine and a rewarding field of knowledge that I have explored and developed at great length for many years. My different works and teachings should reflect precisely that, albeit in varying ways and by providing complementary approaches, especially to those who find in the exploration of the mind and the development of its potential an interest of their own. In this way my words and a committed study of the occult can allow for a unique understanding of modern society, the motivations

✝

and limitations of ordinary people, with the aim of analyzing the logic behind the behavioral patterns of groups and individuals as well as observing the action and inaction of humanity. From their relationships with each other to their dreams, fears and hopes, the occult should provide the advanced adept with a level of clarity that can be used towards the ability to see beyond human limitation and grasp upon the details that manifest a larger picture – the often misunderstood higher understanding of an occult scholar. The system provided within this book when used alongside elements found in my other texts, and in parallel with committed study, attentive contemplation and meditation, should furnish the curious occultist with interesting material to be explored under the banner of psychology and the many unseen secrets of the mind.

Every student or initiate of the Asetian path as a seeker of knowledge and explorer of mysteries faces many challenges and much opposition. Evolving is no simple task and the wiser you become the more misunderstood you shall be, for the vast ocean of humankind dares not taste the forbidden fruit of wisdom and often prefers to trail the path of safety hidden behind the protection of ignorance. To understand means to dare and such an approach is a dangerous aspiration when most do not have the courage to learn beyond the limited walls of their small world. Humanity has long thrived under the notion that if you close your eyes to the unseen it will silently go away, or at the very least will remain latent and unnoticed long enough so that it may be forgotten or no longer a threat. So they live and so they die – in absolute unawareness of the real world and the many truths that await in the dark. That is not an option for Asetianists, who will determinedly face the wingless monsters of despair and defeat any obstacle that stands in their road in order to nurture the inner seed of evolving wisdom; the silent path of the spirit. For that they will ever be condemned, criticized and publicly opposed by those who lack their higher understanding. The ignorant mock those who know more than them but those who know do not take insult for they understand that they simply know no better and mockery is a mirror of fools. Emotion is energy and should be saved and protected for the real threats in your path, not wasted on the envious smoke of limited minds. Take ignorant criticism and insult as a mighty crown and wear it with pride and nobility. Fight with honor. Learn with courage. Understand with wisdom. Only then shall my teachings flourish within your soul and liberate the greatest powers that live inside you.

The contents within this book have been made available to the occult community and students of Asetianism from all over the world in a progressive and non-linear manner for the past five years, which has potentiated the activation of subtle cues that allow us to initiate the superior understanding required to go forward in the study of Asetian mysteries, magick and spirituality. As always, remember that this book is yet another device in the long journey of magick, not the absolute code or a final teaching. It is another weapon in your arsenal of growth.

While some of the presented literary constructs are written sigils of energy and hidden inner power, others reflect much simpler secrets of life, death and the universal laws of nature. In its diversity resides its strength and varied use, with elements dated and published according to deeper significance presented alongside more spontaneous creations moved by lessons taught and learned at the unique moment in time and manifested in my own path, welcoming every Asetianist to drink from this personal road of enlightenment. In such a way this book, my fourth published work outside the secretive walls of my teachings, becomes another tool available to those daring to travel the dangerous road of Asetianism and its dark dungeons of inner potential.

Although this work may benefit anyone interested in magick, the occult and spirituality, even if they are not on the Asetian path, previous study of my other books is recommended to the explorers seeking to venture in the many caves within this tome and uncover the mysteries hiding inside each one, whether laying within golden coffers or sealed behind weathered locks of copper and brass. This is not to say that the Asetian teachings are restrictive, quite the contrary; they are a doorway to many other traditions, cultures and the multitude of knowledge both sacred and mundane available in this world. The Order of Aset Ka has always inspired its inner students and outside followers to explore every form of knowledge and wisdom they can dare touch, and not only through Asetian culture. In this way a learned Asetianist shall fly as an intricate flag of many colors, with insight and understanding of an incredible variety of subjects, reaching as far as the light of the Sun and the darkness of the Moon.

Now complied into a single volume, this system of wisdom has become available to every seeker, student or

✝

initiate of the magickal arts, so that it may be explored in the realms of ritual, meditation, incantation and further teaching. The result is *Words in Silence*, a small grimoire for those who seek to learn the ancient art of spiritual evolution and unfold the forbidden nature of magick through the mysterious power of silent words.

In our modern day and age, with the development of technology and the deceiving sense of empowerment that easy access to information and varying degrees of knowledge provides, many have criticized the Aset Ka for its secrecy and detachment. Often described as elitism and arrogance, such views spawn from the lack of understanding of what drives, enforces and empowers our signature silence and oaths of secrecy. As the author of several Asetian books and teachings I nurture no interest whatsoever in fame and recognition, finding no value in such vain desires. My achievements are held to much higher standards and they are bound to the conquering of growth, wisdom and enlightenment. Those victories are not at the reach of fame and ego, being only sung in the hymns of those who battle in silence, hence conquering the greater fortunes of all. Such uncommon commitment for a high standard and determination in fighting the recurring battle of perfecting your inner and outer arts may be understood as elitism, and under this mindset every Asetian is a proud elitist at heart. This is especially evident in what concerns the mysteries of magick and spirit, as our path can never be explored and understood when approached with the same mind that would seek, study and praise the work of mere dabblers or the mirrors of commercial occultism without a profound sustenance of truth. That is not the way of the Asetians as such a road is not the path of the warrior. In truth, if I would not constantly reject public exposure and the deviant desires of fans and readers, and have my work publicized and reach a much broader audience, I would still be criticized for doing something so opposed to my chosen privacy. As I have made clear in previous books, you cannot please everyone but most importantly nor should you. I would rather embrace criticism while being honest and true to myself, aligned with my nature and ideals, than bask in praise while pretending to be something I am not. Asetian secrecy is not here to please anyone and will remain strong and unbroken despite criticism, but if any genuine seeker finds the secretive nature of our knowledge and the intricate access to our teachings a negative sign of its value, then I am only left to wonder what real wisdom such a person has ever held contact with beyond the grasp of popular magick and basic metaphysics, as every true power fueled by occult knowledge is bound to oaths of secrecy, the art of initiation and vows of responsibility. That is how it has always been on the road to occult science and the way of magick enforced by every mystery school since the dawn of civilization and so it remains today. Believing otherwise is folly. Those seeking easy answers and quick lessons will never accept this but such minds have no place on the path of the wise. By now any student of the mysteries must have realized that Asetians bow to no desire or expectation from others and understand how criticism, insult or defamation hold no power over them. One of the most honest advices that any wise man can give to a new student of the Asetian path and seeker of this ancient culture is to ignore gossip and rumor. Falling for the tales of the lost and the lies of the paranoid is a fate of fools. People lie, manipulate, deceive and pretend, for that is their weakness. They add embellishments of grandeur to their experiences in a desperate attempt to portray to others a greater meaning in their life and existence. It is a facade; a mask of submission to the will of others. Discard all rotten fruit and seek the purity of the source, for only then truth can be found.

After the publishing of my first book and the break of silence that it implied from the Aset Ka after so many years of absolute mystery and confidentiality, some outsiders have stated that a secret Order such as ours should not disclosure esoteric information or release any literary works to the general public – I disagree. There are countless Asetianists spread throughout the world seeking to study this beautiful tradition and other occultists diverse in path and metaphysical approach wondering about Asetian magick, culture and spirituality. As an Order of mysteries with a history of privacy and secrecy, standing on an internal structure of initiation only accessible through the means of direct invitation and not providing any open membership system, it is only but natural that a vast legion of seekers are not actual members of the Aset Ka. It is my belief that such a fact should not be an obstacle to an honest Asetianist learning the intricacies of our path and culture. Even without disclosing an array of initiatory elements, practices and magickal secrets that are internal to the Order, it has been demonstrated that it is still possible to share and initiate those who remain loyal to Aset and the magick of Her children mirrored on the immortal legacy She created. Those who remain strong in their allegiance to

✝

the Aset Ka despite title or membership are worthy of our knowledge, teachings and friendship, proving that their inner quest is not driven by ego or the desire for power, but an honest commitment of the heart carved deep within their soul. Only then shall the ancient serpents of wisdom be willing to share power.

Treacherous obstacles and deceptive illusions raised by outside influences remain a menacing challenge to anyone studying Asetianism outside of our high walls. There is much speculation concerning the Aset Ka and its tradition among those that do not have access to its mysteries and inner workings, in a way that it becomes confusing ground to any truthful seeker of genuine information. It has been inferred that secrecy is the evil cause of all rumor surrounding the Order, however that is inaccurate and an innocent conclusion. It is not privacy, secrecy and mystery causing rumor and the spread of falsehood; it is the ego of those lacking access, information and proper understanding of the Aset Ka but pretending otherwise. Many claim to know secrets and truths of our Order, disseminating misinformation and misunderstanding. It is ironic that someone may criticize the Aset Ka and without any knowledge fantasize about it while using it to feed the ego by convincing others of pretentious access to something they secretly find so alluring and mysterious. The target of hate and unjustified criticism often proves to be an object of hidden desire. Unwillingly and unknowingly, they remain a banner of our power to inspire others and how our silence touches heart, mind and soul, leaving no one indifferent. Those insulting and hating the Asetians and the ones worshipping them accomplish the very same thing: a hymn to our mighty existence, no matter how hard they try to deny and fight the unbreakable nature of our call. From praise and idolatry to hate and insult, none are aware of the inescapable truth that no Asetian seeks worship and attention, constantly dismissing such expressions of admiration – hidden or otherwise – albeit being familiar with all of it for a very long time.

The life of an Asetian is one of magick, beauty and mystery, that being also what we teach and inspire in every Asetianist who freely embraces our spiritual journey and timeless culture. We live all such facets of existence in privacy and honor, as none of us is governed by outside influence or abides to the standards of others. We do not bow; we rise. Such is the strength of the warrior and the mind of the immortal, a trait incomprehensible to those who seek recognition as a mirror of their incompleteness and concealed sorrow. Our path is an endless process of change and growth potentiated by perpetual study, as the crown of all mysteries is infinite and knows no end. The door to such power and the inscrutable nature of our very existence is open to anyone seeking it with a truthful heart and a noble mind but not many will be able to enter and walk our golden road of silver halls and temples of stone, not because we reject their entry but because they limit themselves to their full potential, closing their mind to the openness of possibility and choosing death by oblivion instead.

The cover of this book presents our readers with a photograph of Ancient Egyptian symbolism brought to life through different artifacts, some of which are part of special and unique altars located in currently active Asetian temples. Although simple and aesthetically gracious, such presentation is not random, as some of the objects included hold emotional significance to the Asetians and have relevance in late Asetian history, having been used in actual ritual and magickal work at the Aset Ka, making such inclusion in this work not only rare but also an element of rapport hereby gifted to the Asetianist community and our loyal readers. Additionally, three hand-drawn depictions of Ancient Egyptian artwork by Tânia Fonseca were included in these pages and complement the overall artistic feel and inspiration behind the book, blending with the signature emotion found in the lost art and magick of Kemet, as represented in modern times by the Aset Ka. It is our commitment and long-held belief that the published works we develop represent and personify much more than just books but manifest into actual magickal devices in their own right, each with its very personal identity and pulsating energy. A profound work of magick and ritual exists behind every single book published by the Aset Ka, from its early secretive inception to later stages of artistic development, occult implementation and initiatory discovery. It is a long and arduous journey that it is unlikely to be understood just by the study of the final words but one we believe can be appreciated and felt by the most aware of seekers finding the inner transformation and power that such works preserve and concede. It is a passionate work of love, nurtured not only for the beauty of magick in its purest form and the many lessons contained within, but most importantly as a mirror of our undying commitment to the legacy of Aset in its infinite expressions.

☦

In a compilation of precisely three hundred and seventy three – 373 – individual teachings, each utterance in this book was edited and organized by manifestation date, which is aligned with the original creation or publication moment so that its archetypal intent, will and energy may be preserved and crystalized on this spiritual vehicle of matter that is each Asetian book. Proper references and brief annotations were included in order to easily point the reader toward varying elements of celestial influence and intricate energy signatures such as Full Moons, Equinoxes and other relevant timeframes. *Liber Silentis* can be a tool of ritual and a companion of meditation but it is also importantly a manual for students as well as teachers. May Asetianism be understood as the path where master and apprentice draw swords together and drink of the same chalice.

May the Ka be with your Ba.

Luis Marques
Order of Aset Ka
2014

Asetian Manifesto

To become an Asetian is to die and be reborn.

To forget all you have learned and learn all
you have forgotten.

To be an Asetian is to be blessed with everlasting Love.

1s to be cursed by a never-ending thirst for perfection.

An Asetian is a fierce warrior, a faithful lover and
an eternal concubine. Having the power of the Pharaoh,
the discipline of the Samurai, the knowledge of the Wizard
and the commitment of the Geisha.

Kemet is our Holy Land. The genesis of our immortal Ba.

The Tao is Knowledge. Power is through Blood.

Our Ka is sacred.

Our essence is the storm raindrops in the ocean of mankind,
the winds that blow on their faces and the quakes that
shake the very foundations of their ground.

We are the children of the Gods.
We are the Cursed Ones and the Blessed Ones.

We live in Secret. We live in Silence. And we live Forever...

Liber Silentis

So the violet crown of timeless honor and immeasurable beauty goes forth once more, rising high above the mortal sky as it stood at the emerald dawn of the black lands on its mighty throne of magick.

1

Sometimes the dim veil between
sanity and insanity is perception.

23 August 2009

2

An Asetian never tries to talk louder
than the surrounding crowd.
An Asetian becomes that crowd.

24 August 2009
Asetian Bible

3

The deepest powers are often the
most subtle, something that most
fail to realize.

25 August 2009

4

In the few hours before sunrise the world sparkles as a better place when most are silent and asleep.

26 August 2009

5

Knowledge is a sacred gem that must be conquered, wielded and empowered. To access such gnosis is not a right but a privilege of the evolved.

28 August 2009

6

Thoth paves the silver sky to rise in fullness upon the darkness of the underworld. Nut tenderly misses his empowerment and so do We.

2 September 2009

✝

7

May the Violet Flame be with the ones who are loyal in the night when Thoth rises high and whole to cross the gates of the unseen.

5 September 2009
Full Moon

8

It is safer to face a strong enemy in the field of battle than to fight a war by the side of a weak friend.

6 September 2009
Book of Orion

9

Beauty lies not on the words themselves but in the listener that has the power to understand them.

7 September 2009

✝

10

A day of hidden storms and broken shields. Listen to the silent echoes within the shadow of lost cries and forgotten memories.

9 September 2009

9.9.9

11

When fully united, without ego or weakness, we become the greatest invisible force this world has ever witnessed.

10 September 2009

Book of Orion

12

To become an Asetian is to die and be reborn.

To forget all you have learned and learn all you have forgotten.

12 September 2009

Asetian Manifesto

✝

13

Humans spend more time finding ways to fight and criticize those who they consider a threat than actually learning how to overcome them.

14 September 2009

14

The solitary moveless dance of the Asetians: hidden magick under the prevalence of darkness.

14 September 2009

15

Words are more dangerous than swords and guns.
They reach further and hurt deeper.

27 September 2009

16

Cherish the energies from the deep
and bend them to your will as
Thoth rises once more to empower
in darkness.

4 October 2009
Full Moon

17

Loyalty is a divine gift of the evolved.
Something humanity often places below
their shallow ego
5 October 2009

18

The night is Ours. Rejoicing in the
ethereal realms where We are
kings. Blessed souls of forgotten
immortality. They fear Us in every
grasp.

5 October 2009

✝

19

There is no greater power than
the one others do not believe you
possess.

9 October 2009

20

We live in Secret.
We live in Silence.
And we live Forever...

9 October 2009
Asetian Manifesto

21

Words are sigils that can hide the
coded language of the soul.

12 October 2009

22

In darkness lies a mystery that has the power to shine brighter than true light.

17 October 2009
Book of Orion

23

You don't find Truth but Truth finds you.
19 October 2009
New Moon

24

No matter how hard you try, after the day there will always be a night.

27 October 2009

25

Life is a chance at Evolution.
Overcome yourself and Become.
30 October 2009

26

May Anubis be your loyal guide
through the underworld in the
night where the realms entwine
and the dead we meet.

1 November 2009
Circle of the Dead

27

Thoth blesses Geb with full light.
Vibrant energies in the crossing
through the darkened sky.
3 November 2009
Full Moon

✝

28

An evolved and balanced ego can be a valuable tool for Self. A blinding one remains among the footsteps into oblivion.

6 November 2009

29

May the Ka be with the Ba of those who are Loyal and True.

7 November 2009

30

An Asetian never feels threatened by any force surrounding him.
We had the world on our hands and willingly gave it away...

10 November 2009

✝

31

Humans are naturally scared and confused creatures. They not only fear the unknown as they live fearing themselves.

11 November 2009

32

He who does not cherish life does not deserve to be among the living.

13 November 2009

Book of Orion

33

The power of faith can be a strong force but the power of knowing is even stronger.

14 November 2009

34

Blind is he who innocently strikes the weak apprentice for he is only lowering his guard to the final strike of the master.

15 November 2009

New Moon

35

Truth is not a right to be claimed but a gift for those who are able to conquer it.

18 November 2009

36

Poor are those who have eyes but cannot see...

20 November 2009

37

Light and Darkness. One cannot exist without the other. There is no true master without the power of balance.

25 November 2009

38

You may think that you are not blind but can you see in the dark?

27 November 2009

39

Do not judge others without first judging yourself. There is no true strength without knowing thyself.

28 November 2009

40

The hidden mist of forgotten truth
is not for the mundane eye to see.

29 November 2009

41

Embrace the darkness within and
face the abyss without fear.

2 December 2009
Full Moon

42

Did you ever face Death and let it
stare back at you right in the Eye?

2 December 2009
Full Moon

☥

43

Predator and prey move through silent gestures on a seductive dance of death in the shadow cast by the vultures of the night.

6 December 2009

44

Departures and new beginnings.
Rebirth and Immortality.

7 December 2009

45

To face a demon you must first look inwards and conquer your own darkness.

13 December 2009

46

Blend with the darkness without the blessing of light.

16 December 2009
New Moon

47

The evolved predator can get his prey to willingly enter the forbidden lair, unaware of the despair that lies within.

19 December 2009

48

May you find answers to the mysteries of your inner realities as the cycle shifts and Ra returns.

21 December 2009
Winter Solstice

✝

49

When you feel lost and hopeless just
close your eyes and look deep within.
You will find your compass.

9 January 2010

50

Do not fully believe in what you see
for sometimes only what is not
possible to be seen can be trusted.

10 January 2010

51

The Flame has a fire that not even
death can extinguish. That is the
eternal nature of the Asetian Family,
a bond no human can comprehend.

11 January 2010

†

52

How can you fathom Death if you don't even understand Life?

14 January 2010

53

The darker it gets the easier it becomes for subtle lights to be revealed.

15 January 2010
New Moon

54

There is only one thing worse than a coward and that is a deceptive coward.

17 January 2010

✝

55

The strength of a vampire lies in his soul, as an immortal flame that burns furiously like the devastating forces of nature.

19 January 2010

56

Truth is an ethereal pond hidden among the stars.

23 January 2010
Book of Orion

57

the Kingdom of truth is a twisted realm where reality deceives perception and embraces its purity on the inverted understanding of mortals

27 January 2010
Mirror of Perception

✝

58

Bask in the pale light and ask for the answers that your soul seeks. Inside you lies a puzzle to many mysteries.

30 January 2010
Full Moon

59

Some try so hard to be known and remembered that they fail to realize how insignificant they actually are. Life isn't about fame and recognition but a school of honor and enlightenment.

31 January 2010

60

There is no point in walking if you do not know where you are going.

4 February 2010

61

The silent you become the stronger
you can hear.
The better you stay still the greater
you can see.

7 February 2010

62

There is no Master without being
an eternal student.

There is no Master without the
ability to learn from the ones he
teaches.

There is no Master without the
experience of dying to be reborn...

11 February 2010

63

It hurts less to go forward and be
taken down than to live knowing
that you did not walk.

12 February 2010

64

Even when the face of Thoth is not seen in the sky you still know that he is present.

Seeing does not mean Knowing.

14 February 2010
New Moon

65

To be an Asetian is to be cursed by a never-ending thirst for perfection.

17 February 2010
Asetian Manifesto

66

Life is binary.
You can be a one or a zero.
A warrior or a deserter.
A student or an ignorant.
Aware or blind.
A lover or a coward.

18 February 2010

✝

67

The Tao is Knowledge.
Power is through Blood.
19 February 2010
Asetian Manifesto

68

There is no place like Home.
There is no bond like Family.
There is no sin like Betrayal.
26 February 2010

69

The physical plane is one of deceit.
Constantly strive for awareness.
28 February 2010
Full Moon

✝

70

Violet light can be seen in total darkness but only felt with eyes closed when there is no fear to dim the Flame.

28 February 2010
Full Moon

71

If you have thirst for knowledge always drink from the source where the water is purer.

2 March 2010

72

True power always comes from within.

5 March 2010

☥

73

Your soul is your inner temple.
Your body is but a thin cloak that
you keep changing for a cleaner one
on an eternal ritual of life.
6 March 2010

74

Fire destroys.
The Earth grounds.
Water cleanses.
The Air binds.
But only Blood transforms...
12 March 2010

75

I am the hawk that flies higher; the
darkness that goes forth.
I am the predator that storms from
above; the unformed truth of your
rebirth.
18 March 2010

76

The river of Life will follow its course with or without you. Take your chances carefully for the eternal clock is ticking.

21 March 2010
Spring Equinox

77

Old roots are not dead only if you have the power to pour fresh water on them.

23 March 2010

78

Asetian Souls are like the Pyramids. They have endured the test of time and hold secrets that mankind cannot comprehend.

25 March 2010

✝

79

The night casts shadows upon
our senses in a perfect balance
of darkness and light.
29 March 2010
Full Moon

80

Fear is both a tool and a weapon.
Use it to guide you through a safe
road and to bring nightmares onto
your enemies.

1 April 2010

81

Beware of friends and allies for
only in days of thunder your
enemies shall be revealed.
5 April 2010

82

Fight not to win. Fight to make a stand.
Determination is the key to awareness.
Hunt not to feed. Hunt to learn.
Knowledge is the key to shape the world.
Destroy not to kill. Destroy to transform.
Evolution is the key to immortality.

11 April 2010
Book of Orion

83

In a realm of lies and deceit have
the courage to be someone real.
There is no evolution without being
true to yourself.
23 April 2010

84

Do not fight your enemies. Ignore them.
28 April 2010
Full Moon

85

The very first step in not betraying
someone is to never betray yourself.
The second is to realize that if loyalty
knows an if then it is no loyalty.

7 May 2010

86

When you lie there is only one you
are letting down: yourself.

19 May 2010

87

Every Full Moon a new initiation
begins, destined for those who can
read behind the eyes of Thoth
without falling into his abyss.

27 May 2010
Full Moon

88

The truth that enlightens the evolved often has the power to anger the unaware.

11 June 2010
New Moon

89

Before seeking understanding over the secrets of life first try to uncover your own inner mysteries.

15 June 2010

90

When you see Darkness become the Light and when there is Light become the Darkness.

26 June 2010
Full Moon

91

Never fear those who pretend to
be your enemies for a real danger
always comes in silence.

1 July 2010

92

The deepest cries are those held in
absolute silence.

3 July 2010

93

Three echoes throughout eternity.
The Violet Flame touches heart
and soul of those who were Loyal
and True.

7 July 2010

7.7

94

Pay attention to every word and every gesture for each step echoes in both worlds.

13 July 2010

95

The greatest warrior is not the one with the strongest body but one with the strongest mind.

17 July 2010

96

That which can feed the wise may poison the blind.

24 July 2010

97

An Asetian is both an angel and a demon, with energy capable of healing the deepest wounds and power to take all life at his grasp.

5 August 2010

98

Remember that a soul, just like the phoenix, cannot be reborn without first bursting into flames.

15 August 2010

99

Death is the ultimate initiation for only through its mysteries the Ba can truly Live.

24 August 2010
Full Moon

☦

100

My army is the thunder in the sky and the beasts from the earth, the wind in the air and the tides of the sea. My army is Me.

9 September 2010
Book of Orion
New Moon

101

In the moment when Night equals Day may you remember the importance of balance and equilibrium to an enlightened soul.

23 September 2010
Autumn Equinox
Full Moon

102

The life of a vampire is like a timeless painting. Many souls will come and go in a perpetual cycle but only true artists remain.

22 October 2010
Full Moon

✝

103

Power that needs proof is Doubt.
Power that needs voice is Ego.
Power that betrays is Dishonor.
Power that is afraid is Weakness.
Asetian Power is just Power.
31 October 2010
Circle of the Dead

104

How can mortals survive the test
of time if they cannot even pass
the test of silence?

21 December 2010
Winter Solstice
Full Moon

105

Great strength to claim important
victories; the forging of old bonds
and its powers awoken.
31 December 2010

✝

106

Only in the darkest corners of existence the light cast by our truest Self can be found.

12 January 2011

107

A true Writer cannot die, as the power behind his Words will prevail for ages yet to come.

30 January 2011

108

Be proud of long-due conquered freedom but remain responsible to avoid mistakes from the past.

12 February 2011

✝

109

While it is not our charge to give power to people it remains our responsibility to enlighten them if we do.

20 February 2011

110

Only the Wise can see through the riddles of the universe and grasp upon the simplicity of the answers.

4 March 2011

New Moon

111

Seek your inner darkness for the light of the world is deceptive and transitory.

12 March 2011

112

When ego is conquered and our honor raised to everlastingness we reach a plenitude that leaves us with nothing left to fear.

19 March 2011
Full Moon

113

Thoth dances through the body of Nut with a Light that threatens to blind those who are too scared to See.

19 March 2011
Full Moon

114

It is of unquestionable beauty how after so many lifetimes we can still feel such an intense passion for Life as if it was our first.

31 March 2011

✝

115

Asetianism is spiritual liberation, the most profound form of Freedom through the power of Knowing. Who lacks such understanding does not know the Violet path at all.

17 April 2011
Full Moon

116

A wise vampire can hunt treacherous preys by allowing them to believe that they are actually being predators.

7 May 2011

117

Deciding the fate of others is not a pleasant experience. It is a necessary power and responsibility of leadership that no one should seek.

17 May 2011
Full Moon

118

Words are poison, potion and elixir.
Choose wisely which ones to drink...

24 May 2011

119

The secret Light of the Lady echoes
in the deep like the sound of drums
against the hands of giants.
Once more We claim our victory.

11 June 2011

120

The initiate replicates the ancient
mystical art with a steady hand and a
focused mind as a surgeon of nature,
the sculptor of souls...

1 July 2011
New Moon

✝

121

Sing the hymn of honor, joy and passion on the embrace of Aset, Her legacy and beloved children.

7 July 2011

7.7

122

In a world filled with blinding light may we proudly continue to be the darkness that preserves its mystery.

7 July 2011

7.7

123

Understanding is a power greater than any form of knowledge, manifesting as a harbinger of wisdom.

15 July 2011

Full Moon

✝   73

124

Fear... Such a small harmless word yet able to move so many. Once you give in to fear you have already lost.

26 July 2011

125

Orion glows strong on the dark sky of the temple, carrying the same message it did so many ages ago.

18 August 2011

126

The fall of ghosts is written in the tales from the rise of giants.

28 August 2011
New Moon

127

A true spiritual leader teaches not
only with his words but also through
his silence.

7 September 2011

128

Silence allows for fools to wonder,
for the weak to fear, for cowards to
run and for the loyal to awaken.

7 September 2011

129

You cannot fight Union, Loyalty and
Love with lies, envy and anger.

19 September 2011

✝

130

Life is too beautiful and meaningful to be wasted fighting what you can never defeat or comprehend. Cherish its treasures and ease your pain.

19 September 2011

131

Asetianism embraces the path of darkness through a definitive quest for liberation by unfolding the greater mystery: yourself.

29 September 2011

132

Knowing Life is to know the Spirit. Knowing the Spirit is to know Life.

10 October 2011

✝

133

Servitude to the ego is an echo of
a life of slavery. Break the chains
and rise above!
17 October 2011

134

Only a fool tries to hunt down a
lion by throwing grains of sand.

26 October 2011

New Moon

135

We that live between the veil of
both worlds offer a moment of
silence for those that have fallen.
In darkness we honor their soul.
31 October 2011
Circle of the Dead

✝

136

The silent Hawk always stares into the confused eyes of the fallen before they fall...

22 November 2011

137

She taught us how to Love, without fear or weakness, and that forever remains a banner of our Family.

1 December 2011

138

The voice of immortality can only sing to the eyes of purity.

12 December 2011

✝

139

Who seeks fantasy and ego shall find delusion and disappointment. Who seeks growth and enlightenment shall find wisdom and rebirth.

31 December 2011

140

With power to inspire and bring nightmares each Asetian is a candle forgotten in the wind, permanently touching all life around him.

7 January 2012

141

Freedom is one of the best spiritual tools. You claim the merit for your evolution but if you fall you only have yourself to blame.

23 January 2012
New Moon

†

142

Can you see Orion reflected in
your inner desert?

7 February 2012
Full Moon

143

Understanding hides in absolute
darkness while hatred finds its
altar only in the light.
21 February 2012
New Moon

144

In life we are not walking towards
a goal or place. We are walking
towards ourselves.

8 March 2012
Full Moon

†

145

Rest on my wings for I am death
and burn in my fire for I am life.
6 April 2012
Full Moon

146

We can hold responsibility over our
words and the power they unleash but
never for how others misinterpret their
use and meaning.

15 April 2012

147

When blessed with true wings you
do not care to prove how well you
can fly.
21 April 2012
New Moon

148

At the dawn of despair we shaped
mountains and served terror.

21 May 2012
New Moon

149

Bask in the light of all abominations
for only when going through the
gates of the abyss you shall find
your answer.

27 May 2012
Book of Orion

150

To reach the gates of transformation
you must first cross the desert of the
soul.

15 June 2012

✝

151

Liber Aeternus.
The law of Three. Initiation into the
mysteries of Orion comes forth.
3 July 2012
Full Moon

152

When the laws of Maat are in balance
and the Word is placed upon the altar
of Truth, the Universe bends to our
own microcosm.

7 July 2012

7.7

153

Observation is a tool of the Wise, a
power of the Initiator and a compass
of the Conqueror.
18 July 2012
New Moon

✝

154

The snake is a symbol of the evolving soul. As it sheds the skin so must the spirit perpetually be renewed to retain ethereal youth.

27 July 2012

155

Someone who has never lost and that has never fallen is not equipped to succeed.

Embrace change. Fear nothing.

7 August 2012

156

To survive in the jungle of life you must unleash your wild inner beast.

31 August 2012

✝

157

The beauty of Truth is that it always
finds a way for it is the only path of
nature.

7 September 2012

158

Every genius mind through the limited
eye of fools is seen as insane.

18 September 2012

159

May the light of wisdom intertwine
with your darkest energies.

29 September 2012
Full Moon

160

There is hidden dark beauty in imperfection for it is through its influence that uniqueness manifests.

7 October 2012

161

Strength when enforced only through extremes is a sign of a limited mind.

15 October 2012

New Moon

162

Poison does not hold sway over the accomplished occultist as the wise know how to craft their own elixir.

29 October 2012

Full Moon

✝

163

Nut blesses the body of Geb
with her precious tears of Life.
6 November 2012

164

Only those who do not seek
power but commit to the quest
of understanding can stare both
in the eye.

13 November 2012
New Moon

165

Perpetually misunderstood, the
occultist is the scholar of life and
death, the scientist of the unseen
and the seeker of all mysteries.
25 November 2012

166

One is only complete when embracing every corner of inner nature, from the brightest seed of Self to the darkest dungeon of evil.

4 December 2012

167

By studying the secrets of long gone history we can grasp into pieces of our own inner mysteries.

12 December 2012
New Moon

168

Clouds of wisdom conceal the spoils from silent battles of fallen leaves.

17 December 2012

169

The subtle seed of Asetianism can only be planted deep into the rich soil of the soul.

21 December 2012
Book of Orion
Winter Solstice

170

Never trust a path that teaches you not to try, experiment and question. Exploration remains one of the most powerful tools of understanding.

23 December 2012

171

Be an explorer of the unseen, a committed student of the mysteries within. Rise not as lost thread of conceit but as a master of Self.

23 December 2012

✝

172

There are no rules but those of the heart. There are no laws but those of imagination.

25 December 2012

173

The deepest bonds are not celebrated with words or gestures but felt in the silence of the heart.

31 December 2012

174

The delusional live in Netzach thinking of Tiphareth but the deceitful often cannot see beyond Malkuth while dreaming of Yesod.

3 January 2013

†

175

If you are constantly seeking for the approval of others you are living a life of no significance.

11 January 2013
New Moon

176

Light is an expression of ego and fear in disguise. Darkness represents its absence without expectation.

14 January 2013

177

There is a world within your mind that is far greater than that of the manifest Universe.

23 January 2013

†

178

Many are ashamed to question but it is the incarnated condition of doubt that moves the mind forward in order to learn something new.

27 January 2013
Full Moon

179

Foul voices who never felt the weight of a sword speak of death and courage with an arrogance that is unworthy of blood spilled in honor.

6 February 2013

180

Never profess an ideology that you do not have the courage to live by.

8 February 2013

✝

181

Souls of darkness hidden beneath the silent cloak of mortality are often the spark of inspiration that shape the course of history.

21 February 2013

182

Give in, wholeheartedly, to the song of nature and your inner beauty...

25 February 2013

Full Moon

183

To stand a victor is easy but to fight when defeat charges ahead is what defines courage.

3 March 2013

✝

184

Writing is timeless spiritual art;
Words, primordial magick.
Magus, writer and reader are one:
the craftsman of worlds.

7 March 2013

185

Spiritual initiation is the transcendent
path of the phoenix, where you liberate
yourself to die in order to be reborn.

11 March 2013
New Moon

186

The awakened vampire is a spiritual
chimera, conquering inner light and
mastering darkness between worlds
– immortal spirit within mortal shell.

15 March 2013

187

Magick is not the attaining of power but
mastery of what hides within.

20 March 2013
Spring Equinox

188

In a vain modern world inspired by
conflict and competition, an Asetian
mind committed to loyalty and honor
is bound to be misunderstood.

23 March 2013

189

Intuition is a powerful ally. Look into
the lidless eye and listen to its seductive
voice without hesitation.

27 March 2013
Full Moon

✝

190

You don't have to justify your beliefs to anyone! Openly celebrate them without fear of judgement and find the missing spark.

30 March 2013

191

By making Asetianism so illusive, the initiate truly seeking to follow it only has one way to go: inwards.
4 April 2013

192

False teachers pose threat only to fools. They bare a message with rotten fruit and speak of a tree that has no seed.

10 April 2013
New Moon

†

193

Desire for power instead of worthiness
in its higher use is the seed that burns
empires to the ground.

15 April 2013

194

Bonds forged by the magickal fire of
the Violet Flame have the perpetual
quality of spiritual immortality.

18 April 2013

195

Who once boldly or silently protected
the black land of Egypt is bound to
fight for it ever again as such Love is
stronger than time.

18 April 2013

☦

196

All must be free to seek their own individual path and unlock inner truth. Limitations are not imposed by others but raised by self.

22 April 2013

197

Understanding of Asetian will transcends the realm of mortal consciousness. Attempting to see beyond the portal of our abyss is futile.

24 April 2013
Full Moon

198

Any force can be broken with the understanding of the right tool.

29 April 2013

✝

199

Prayer is not the reciting of established scripture but to touch the divine with your very soul.

2 May 2013

200

Extraordinary people are not governed by the ideals of ordinary men.

7 May 2013

201

To embrace the lies of others for personal gain is not only expressive of a weak character but also the mark of a coward.

9 May 2013

†

202

Loving self is not the same as worshipping self.

One mirrors confidence while the other speaks of delusion.

10 May 2013
New Moon

203

Not everyone survives the influence of Asetianism as its truth violently shatters ego in a rebirth that only the strong can overcome.

12 May 2013

204

Trust not those who speak of Kether without first being accepted in Binah.

16 May 2013

☥

205

Do not trust a teacher who raises limitations in your quest but embrace the master who advises you to study the work of his opposers.

19 May 2013

206

The apparently simpler metaphysical rituals often imply the most advanced mindset. The most advanced magickal processes rely on your surrender to simplicity.

21 May 2013

207

Inability to understand tradition or succeed at practice does not constitute evidence of its limitation but of your own.

24 May 2013

208

Our Empire is no longer felt on the sand of a desert or the flow of a river, nor confined to the boundaries of land. It became one of Spirit.

25 May 2013
Full Moon

209

Art differs from entertainment in the sense that it aims to represent the embodiment of subtle beauty without the influence of ego.

26 May 2013

210

The inner need for approval and recognition is inversely proportional to the level of mastery.

31 May 2013

✝

211

Understanding is the weapon of the Wise.
Explore it fearlessly.
Use it openly with caution.
2 June 2013

212

We fight ignorance with wisdom, fear with silence and weakness with strength.

5 June 2013

213

If the focus of life is misplaced on reaching objectives the purpose of existence is missed for its beauty hides in the journey.
10 June 2013

†

214

History is written by men of power – a perspective, sometimes a vendetta. The truth of the people is often untold, surviving only as myth.

11 June 2013

215

There is more to learn from the will of a dedicated student than in the advice of a pretentious teacher.

14 June 2013

216

People smile, agree and connect to conform, be accepted and avoid judgment. Webs of lies in the eye of those who were not born to follow.

17 June 2013

✝

217

Sometimes not causing pain requires greater strength than to masterfully swing the sword.

19 June 2013

218

Do not fear touching the blinding energy of Ra but use it guardedly in your favor without setting your soul ablaze.

21 June 2013
Summer Solstice

219

Three is Magick.
Seven is Sacred.

23 June 2013
Full Moon

220

The weak prey on the innocent and needy in a spectacle that exposes their own limitations.

27 June 2013

221

When you close your eyes to embrace the selfless nature of Asetian loyalty you shall discover the final temple.

30 June 2013

222

We speak the language of Fire and our words have the gentle touch of flames.

5 July 2013

✝

223

For we are darkness and speak Her name.

7 July 2013

7.7

New Moon

224

Rising fast means nothing when someone is rising to emptiness. Do not seek fame as accomplishment; conquer honor and wisdom instead.

14 July 2013

225

Do not ignore the alchemical medicine pouring behind an honest smile.

17 July 2013

226

Only the strong can commit to a path that would take lifetimes of learning. Asetian fire breaks the weak and nurtures the strong.

19 July 2013

227

Someone who does not accept criticism will never be able to improve. Evolution is the path to mastery.

22 July 2013
Full Moon

228

Do not practice magick.
Become magick.

24 July 2013

†

229

The experienced commander understands how conceding defeat in a battle may present opportunity to win the war.

26 July 2013

230

Being capable of unspeakable things, vampires make no use of their abilities lightly for they seek no recognition. Just like a master sensei who knows how to kill is less likely to resort to such skills than the ordinary man.

30 July 2013

231

Asetianism expresses the inner art of honoring Aset through Her spiritual legacy as She is the essence of the violet bond that unites us.

6 August 2013
New Moon

☥

232

Experience through diversity gives birth to enlightened tolerance, only rightfully chastised in the service of justice and honor.

9 August 2013

233

Inspiration is cyclical, flowing to the tides of an endless ocean. Whoever believes it to be permanent has yet to hear its fluid song.

11 August 2013

234

The smallest of flames can conceal the heat to ignite the greatest fires.

14 August 2013

235

Words can be deceiving. Observe
choices, behaviors and patterns
instead. Truth lies in details.

18 August 2013

236

Someone clouded by ego and obsessed with
delusions of grandeur becomes exposed
among the most limited of mortals.

Each cheer of the crowd, blind as the mere
object of false admiration, echoes a hymn at
their insignificance.

Embrace darkness within and conquer
silent deeds worthy of immortal ages, not
the vain whispers of those in decay.

20 August 2013
Full Moon

237

The mind is a creator of worlds,
a most mighty magickal tool.

25 August 2013

✝

238

If you dare looking into dark places
you may not like what you see.

29 August 2013

239

For millennia humanity has searched
for the divine to feed their spiritual
hunger, yet it still fails to recognize
the sacredness within.

2 September 2013

240

If someone willingly chooses to
close eyes at the waters of truth
do not blow air on his face but let
the fire of death teach him.

5 September 2013
New Moon

✝

241

I teach people not to find magick in religion, dogma or the creations of mankind but in the intuition of their inner seed.

Those seeking quick, easy and safe results shall never understand my methods or the nature of my magick.

7 September 2013

242

Only someone who does not feel special exhibits the need to convince others of their uniqueness.

11 September 2013

243

There is no greater teacher than death.

16 September 2013

244

Who is lost can ever be found and all that is hidden does not live forever for eternal lie shall never be bound.

20 September 2013
Full Moon

245

A master lays the tools so that you may carve the path, it does not force you to believe for no truth can be imposed.

21 September 2013

246

To learn and live or to give up and wither is a choice every seeker will have to face at the doors of Khepri.

23 September 2013
Autumn Equinox

✝

247

Be suspicious of those who appear
with a thousand friends for the gift
of friendship is a rare flower under
selfless bloom.

26 September 2013

248

Your path cannot be broken by the
actions of others but only through
the inaction of Self.

29 September 2013

249

Elder magick cannot be contained,
only unleashed.

1 October 2013

250

Of all arts those serving the ego are the less relevant and consequentially the ones that lack the quality of immortality.

5 October 2013
New Moon

251

Danger lies not on the larger arm but in the smallest shadow.
9 October 2013

252

Our river still flows to the sound of music from the Gods, as blood carrying life to the black lands of old.

12 October 2013

253

Do not let growth be hindered by distractions. Such demons can only be banished through the fiery wand of your will.

15 October 2013

254

True strength is manifestly silent but the blind are chained to the unawareness that loudness mirrors their weakness.

19 October 2013
Full Moon

255

Ego establishes the boundaries of your being. When removed you become endless.

23 October 2013

256

To craft the hidden art you must accept in the eye of thunder that only when alone you become magick.

27 October 2013

257

Life should be a celebration of the moment but also a conscious preparation for the initiation of death.

30 October 2013
Circle of the Dead

258

When we look closely there is magick everywhere, like a subtle clock taming the tides of time.

3 November 2013
New Moon

259

Only honesty is worthy of our respect.

6 November 2013

260

Secrets live not in the symbols for the symbols live within you and you are the secret.

8 November 2013

261

A mystical path requires courage as you must take a first step of faith so that the second may be of science.

12 November 2013

262

Someone incapable of love will often attempt to diminish those who celebrate their passion without fear.

16 November 2013
Full Moon

263

They raised fortresses where honesty is burned and valor diminished as falsehood became nurtured and vanity worshiped.

19 November 2013

264

When wielding elemental Fire do not blend the fluidity of Water unless you are willing to drink from the unheard sacrifice.

19 November 2013

✝

265

Did you ever listen to the world through
the sound of a storm or seen its magick
in the eye of a falcon?
Have you ever felt it through the dance
of the wind or uncovered its mysteries in
the timeless words of poets?
22 November 2013

266

Only a soul with scars can speak of
pain, strength and fear.

24 November 2013

267

Answer honesty with kindness, respect
with dignity and rudeness with class.
27 November 2013

268

Ignorance seeking to ridicule sapience
is a recurring brand of a futile society
enslaved by weakness.

29 November 2013

269

When you trust the invisible over
illusions of matter thou shall be
ready to cross our gates.

1 December 2013

270

In matters of spirit anything but
excellence is insignificant.

4 December 2013

New Moon

✝

271

The tome of evolution is found only by
the scribe of patience.

5 December 2013

272

Any soul that dishonorably scars
a seed of Aset is bound to an
inescapable truth: it may take one
day or a lifetime but fire awaits.

9 December 2013

273

Destiny is the map of every individual
choice in a unique roadmap of fate
defined by the sum of your actions and
inactions. Choose wisely.

12 December 2013

274

Creation and destruction are dangerous yet essential catalysts of evolution – the machinery of renewal.

14 December 2013

275

Devouring through sacred fire brings forth the tears of life as children of initiation.

14 December 2013

276

Do not speak of demons, evil and terror to instigate dread for the fabric of darkness is silent and nameless.

17 December 2013
Full Moon

✝

277

The fall of deceit. Rest assured that a magus who fancifully exhibits his title is likely to need your wisdom more than he can ever teach.

19 December 2013

278

Magick is entirely selfless. It serves no desire for validation nor bends to ego. Magick is, nonetheless, undeniably arrogant. It does not listen to opinion nor does it care for judgement.

21 December 2013
Winter Solstice

279

When winter visits your temple do not curse the temper of rain but embrace its cleansing touch as it softly kisses your skin.

25 December 2013
Call of Winter

†

280

To remain idle is easy but to break thunder upon the face of injustice defines valor.

28 December 2013

281

Be one of the rare few to carve a mark in this world that you would be proud to leave upon your passing.

31 December 2013

282

Celebrate the past, embrace the present and seize the future.

1 January 2014
New Moon

283

The greatest heroes are not celebrated
in public for they discard recognition,
conquering historical deeds discreetly
in silence.

5 January 2014

284

Someone unwilling to fight for his
passions and dreams deserves not
having them fulfilled.

7 January 2014

285

The seventh night to all walking this
violet road of Her mysteries.

7 January 2014

†

286

In time everything putrid is brought to surface and the rotten stumble into the light.

10 January 2014

287

The greatest mistake you can do on the path of the living is to take anything for granted. Only impermanence prevails.

13 January 2014

288

There is no ego that we cannot break. Only upon our eternal mirror of silence can your will truly be revealed.

14 January 2014

†

289

Asetians stand unbroken by the passing of frozen winds as old alliances fall and the tides of history are carved in purple stone.

16 January 2014
Full Moon

290

Leave judgement on the chosen life of others to those without a fulfilling life of their own.

18 January 2014

291

Selfless union forged by trust is one of the most indestructible forces this realm has ever seen.

20 January 2014

†

292

Warriors make deliberate use of contemplation before moving pieces on the board of life, unlike fools who act loudly without thought.

23 January 2014

293

Detachedly prune your inner garden of all weeds that hinder its blooming and pour poison on the crawling worms that seek your fruit.

25 January 2014

294

A spell is not a mental afterthought or the result of mystical illusion. It is energy given purpose and set in motion by conscious will.

28 January 2014

✝

295

Both love and hate yield great power,
however only one leads to the ancient
gates of immortality.

30 January 2014
New Moon

296

You cannot fight that which remains
unseen for an enemy daring to strike
upon us must first learn how to
enslave smoke with bare hands.

1 February 2014

297

The strongest magick is not attained
through the constructs of ritual, being
manifested into reality by the unsung
will of the heart.

3 February 2014

298

When the temple of the Elders becomes silent the seed of intent is revealed.

6 February 2014

299

The ecstasy of supreme liberation is not a sin of carnal allegiance but the expression of our innermost sexual divinity.

9 February 2014

300

Speak your mind.
Act on your ideals.
Trust your instincts.
Live your dreams.
Never surrender.
Ignore hate, envy and dishonest criticism.

11 February 2014

✝

301

Only the weak are content with what
is to be found at surface.

13 February 2014

302

The silver crown of Thoth serves the
war banners of wisdom under the
rule of forgotten pharaohs without
name.

14 February 2014
Full Moon

303

When you have been judged by time
and tested by the undying fire no
word of mortals holds power over
you.

15 February 2014

☥ 133

304

Arguing with fools is useless. Allow them to speak and their words become a banner of their incomplete self.

17 February 2014

305

Anyone who explores the occult, magick or spirituality as a competition in any possible form is bound to inevitable failure.

20 February 2014

306

Trusting real initiations to be breakable or its bonds not eternal is one of the most dangerous mistakes an occultist can do.

23 February 2014

✝

307

We celebrate truth in a world of liars.

25 February 2014

308

Deluded minds seeking the apotheosis of self-deification only expose their blindness towards the divine within.

27 February 2014

309

A dragon can only be awoken by fire.

1 March 2014

New Moon

†

310

Thoughts may define character but only actions carve the valley of honor.

4 March 2014

311

With power it becomes easy to claim justice with bare hands and determined will but who are we to condemn others to torment?

How many unspeakable sins have we not committed ourselves, in this life or any before, only to rise beyond any scar?

Be wary of easy assumptions and the quick judgement typical of a mortal mind for even the very wise restrain from using such dagger.

7 March 2014

312

Servants of the hippopotamus in the Nile may adamantly not bend the knee yet what does not bend can be broken.

9 March 2014

✝

313

Sometimes only the painful light of thunder can illuminate the machinery of wisdom.

12 March 2014

314

Harmony is born out of the seed of contrast under the mantle of duality.

14 March 2014

315

Without the grace of winter you cannot appreciate the warm smile of the sun and without the thirst of summer you cannot dance in the rain.

15 March 2014

✝

316

On the motherly cradle of Nun
endures a devastating mystery
that only the Queen holds its
daunting key.

16 March 2014
Full Moon

317

As a living force of transformation
and renewal there is no shame in
change for only the unbending rock
never grows.

20 March 2014
Spring Equinox

318

When grasping beyond the limits
of flesh raised by blindness of
physical existence it becomes
undeniable that we are infinite.

23 March 2014

†

319

May those seeking dreams of a
pretentious heaven follow their
deluded hope as we courageously
embrace immortal hell.

27 March 2014

320

To find the true thoughts hidden
behind masks and barriers we must
pierce deeply into the understanding
of their nightmares.

30 March 2014

New Moon

321

Disregard for the natural world in
its infinite expressions is the stain
of a society that does not realise
its pathetic insignificance.

1 April 2014

†

322

Magick not empowered by feelings is not magick at all.

4 April 2014

323

The ability to feel is tied to the fabric of your soul and feelings are not just chemical reactions but energy given form.

5 April 2014

324

Remember that how you see the world is not necessarily reality. What you see is a distorted perspective filtered through your perception.

8 April 2014

✝

325

The everlasting bond of Family finds
its sacredness not in blood but on the
willing heart of the soul.
The Ib of the Ba.
11 April 2014

326

Never forget that there is more to learn
from sorrow than from happiness. Only
balance creates a complete life.

14 April 2014
Full Moon

327

If you lie about someone as an
attempt to discredit his words you
are not proving them false but only
revealing your fear of their power.
18 April 2014

✝

328

Certain eyes see in Asetians the gentler souls ever created while others find in them the personification of evil given flesh. Perception. Which mirrors the truth beneath our mantle of mystery?

20 April 2014

329

Many get lost seeking for answers they may never find, forgetting to live and enjoy the blessings already bestowed upon them.

24 April 2014

330

Fitting in is a quest of fools. Being accepted a hope of the weak.

Embrace your uniqueness notwithstanding opposition and criticism.

27 April 2014

†

331

We are horse and rider; the banner
high on the mountain. Chill of the
forest and shadow in the dark. We
are sword, steel and death.

30 April 2014
New Moon

332

Eternity is only achieved through
the perpetual experience of now.

4 May 2014

333

Fire destroys the weak and nourishes
the strong.

7 May 2014

334

No human power can burn the armies carrying flags soaked in red for only the flaming sword of immortals can scar their false crown.

9 May 2014

335

If someone insults or spreads lies concerning you it speaks more about them than it does about you.

12 May 2014

336

When we bleed we bleed as One.

15 May 2014

Full Moon

✝

337

Who wields the greatest power
finds no service in its exhibition.

18 May 2014

338

A lost soul is not an abandoned
soul. Hidden beauty and forgotten
truth forever concealed until the
violet storm that can set it free.

24 May 2014

339

Most can only understand life in
shallow waters while we command
fleets through major storms at the
abyss.

28 May 2014
New Moon

✝

340

Empress of silver light, immortal Queen that brings empires to its knees and raises armies to the height of infinity.

1 June 2014

341

Drawing inspiration from recognition is a common sign on the absence of art upon the birth of commerce and ephemeral gratification.

5 June 2014

342

To be immortal is to start anew. Ancient flame in renewed shell, remembering to be One again.

9 June 2014

†

343

Nature does not listen to the sound of envy and hate; it only sings to the voice of silence.

13 June 2014
Full Moon

344

Not only physical experiences allow us to live the greatest stories. Often the very subtle hold the unexpected power to redraw our lives.

18 June 2014

345

Asetians are proud to be a small Family for never in history so few rose above so many.

21 June 2014
Summer Solstice

346

When summer visits your temple do not hide from the sun but master its cleansing flame as it arrogantly burns your skin.

22 June 2014
Call of Summer

347

When making a promise, commit to it through life and death. If your word loses power you become nothing.

29 June 2014

348

My soul is my compass. My inner master. The map of my past, candle of my present and omen of my future.

3 July 2014

✝

349

Exiled from the sand that blessed their
sunrise and unbound from the mortal
coil of eternal slumber they bent stone
and forged an empire.

7 July 2014

7.7

350

Those who succeed are not the ones
that never do mistakes but those who
never give up and that their mistakes
only make them fight harder.

9 July 2014

351

A species that does not respect nature
and its unquestionably superior power
shall never be respected in return.

12 July 2014

Full Moon

☦

352

Asetianism is not about power, it is about knowing. However, knowing often is power.

16 July 2014

353

The despair of those who hide elusive sadness beneath masked smiles and empty laughs is often evident as screams to all but themselves.

20 July 2014

354

We unleash fire that can burn time and forge the invisible bonds of immortality.

25 July 2014

✝

355

To condemn and criticize what you do
not understand and know nothing about
is merely a futile exercise of ignorance.

27 July 2014

New Moon

356

Immortal drops forgotten on an
ocean of living mortality.
Unawakened love.

31 July 2014

357

Only those freely wielding their words
unbroken may sing among the stars.

3 August 2014

358

When facing dishonor there is nothing
as powerful as indifference.

5 August 2014

359

A beating heart veils the silent tune
of the last untouched stone.

7 August 2014

360

At the ancient crossing where Her
name remains unspoken a lost token
reveals the undying words of silver.

7 August 2014

†

361

Those obsessed with power will
remain the ones lacking it.

9 August 2014

362

The most delicate alchemy allows
for the transformation of pain and
sorrow into wisdom.

10 August 2014
Full Moon

363

The ignorance of those who
misunderstand your world and
existence is commonly echoed
through judgment, cynicism, fear
and lies.

12 August 2014

364

Through pristine valleys along the road unseen the thread of starlight peeks beneath the golden door.

13 August 2014

365

When the beast within rests under the delicate balance of your willpower there is no enemy that can break you.

14 August 2014

366

Cowardice and laziness are common triggers behind the conscious or unconscious refusal of most to think for themselves.

16 August 2014

☥

367

Strength cannot be glimpsed on the fabric of your body for it only becomes visible upon the mirror of your thoughts, choices and actions.

16 August 2014

368

When lost in the dark instead of turning on the light seek that which may teach you how to see in its absence.

17 August 2014

369

You cannot teach honor and loyalty to someone without character and a strong personality.

19 August 2014

370

Do not feed shallow tales to a monster nor teach it the laws of mortal men. A demon must not be tamed for it needs only to be unleashed...

20 August 2014

371

Never mistake silence for idleness and unawareness...

22 August 2014

372

On Her seductive halls of truth the violet fire burns everlastingly, echoing the primordial anthem that carries the untold mystery of old.

23 August 2014

†

373

So the word is sealed and the road of five revealed.

23 August 2014

The Call of the Warrior

In silence the storm gathers
For in darkness our name is spoken
The gaping pit of lost nightmares
Rising high where it cannot be found

We shall ride the raging monsters
Bringing the Sun unto our domain
Crushing down with one thousand spears
Raining flame above thy name

To raise the Moon on stellar heights
Unleashing wisdom in trails of silver
For Thoth has come and Nut remained
Our army calling in timeless trumpets

We cause pain and heal the flame
Storming the enemies of Her name
Without fear or a thread of shame
Serving the empire in hidden game

We are the violet legion
The sword that cuts in the dark
A terror that goes forth
The chill in the long night

Her crown, a beacon of hope
Cold skin, the gracious dove
Her hair, forgotten tales
Menacing eyes, the strength of us

Shining deeds seek not the light
Ancient lore that became legend
A song in the dreams of mortals
Terrifying secret unknown to men

By conquering fire we forged a fate
Through mighty stone we crushed all thought
In solitude we curse the desert
For in Her womb our bonds revive

We are the warriors of death
The sages of immortal life
Our shields are crafted of sorrow
Our swords made of shadow and light

We hunt the souls and brand their call
We claim life and give it anew
Taming dragons with whips of silence
We fly above your world in unseen view

†

The word is sealed.
Em Hotep.

They were only Three.

Yet, they moved a nation.

They were only Seven.

Yet, they conquered the desert.

They became endless.

Yet, they were forgotten.

They became legend.

Then, they were remembered.

Liber Aeternus III.3

Lightning Source UK Ltd.
Milton Keynes UK
UKHW012046240921
391136UK00002B/705

9 789899 569430